Empty Shoe Conversation Oeuvre

MT Hsu

First edition December 2020

Cover design: Angela Ni
Back cover portrait: IG @natalie_photoart

ISBN 978-0-5788-2014-9 (paperback)
ISBN 978-0-5788-2015-6 (ebook)

Dedicated to those that inspire

Empty Shoe

I told my friend I was going to write a book called Empty Shoe
Self-named
Ironically, I truly believe the glass is half empty
I stare at the glass as one stares at a cloudless sky for rain
Fake it until you make it
There's no way to fake the physiology of water
Eventually it may become foggy
But my eyes are the ones that are tired
Or ex deus machina, there is no glass or water.

Everyone writes books these days
We are all so very important
We all have something to say
Like all trees falling all at once in the forest
Maybe the source of climate change
Can't we be more like a circle of dominoes
Let's be each other's company instead.

There are so many subway stories
I like to smile at other people's dogs and children
I don't like to smile at anyone else
I have *resting bitch face*
An active Napoleon complex in my mind
In actuality, it is *resting upset face*
People smile at me instead
I avoid eye contact, stranger danger
I am not upset; it must be the glass's fault.
My inner feminist at her best
A small girl squeaking, 'I'm hardcore!'
I may be little but I will bite you
Shakespeare was referring to me

This is not chick-lit, there's no love story
I will however adamantly root for your love life
But more importantly, your inner feminist.

I am very curious and that will get me into trouble
I ask questions to your question
I want to discover the ultimate truth
Where the growth becomes doubt
The world is colorful with hues
There is only infinity
We do not like what we do not know
But then there is significance and statistics
We must all become better statisticians
Then we will know real truth.

Human life is experienced through ourselves
The colorful world that we all see differently
We have perceived connections
I like to imagine our real selves lie in a different dimension
Unaware of our physical neighbors
While here, we are also unaware of those who pass by
The world is vast
We live within the bubble we chose to be in.

Denial is a funny thing that exists outside of ourselves
If I were in denial, I wouldn't be denying
However it is easy to see being in denial
Even easier to see others
A gentle way to put truth onto a spectrum
Another form of empathy and perceived connection.

I have trouble watching tv and movies
I get bored when there isn't something interesting

Someone thinks I should get checked for ADHD
This will be written proof of her diagnosis
I am in denial because testing costs too much time and money
Knowing would not add or take away from my current life.

Things that spark my interest:
Train wrecks with no real damage
Dumpster fires with no consequence
Gossip until I think about humanity
Guilty pleasures until reality hits
It's a pretty nice bubble I'm in.

The million-dollar question
Would I change with money?
Yes, I would have more time
And more things that I don't need
Therefore I don't need the millions
But I would have the power to change the world
And I would no longer be in denial.

I am too blunt
This all may be too honest
I will really have to hide at my real self's location
But this is what I need at the moment
The perceived human connection
While being self indulgent with my importance
An attempt to catch your attention and share
Standing on my little shoebox
With no remorse in failure or success
But hopeful in the positive direction
The glass is definitely foggy.

Ripple Effect Confessions

I sometimes just blame it on the subway system.

I feel guilty when it is the perfect temperature, and I turn on the fan and sleep with a blanket.

I'm not completely truthful when I complained to you that I don't have money and then order discounted clothing to wear 2 seasons away.

I judge you for taking the last piece when I hate wasting food and fervently will not take the last piece myself.

Your food will always taste better than mine.

We bumped into each other, and you spilled your entire cold brew latte. I don't know you, but I ran away. My first thought was that I didn't have the money to buy you a new one.

I set up dates, then immediately and continue to regret that decision until the very last minute, and then go and have a good time, and then feel bad that I really didn't want to go in the first place.

I think I really did sleep with you once because you brought me flowers. I sold myself cheap.

We have both healed nicely, but I still feel bad for breaking your heart; I broke mine too.

I prayed everyday that I would die at the age of 25 when I was a preteen. Some part of me still sees that inner shadow.

I ignore most beggars and homeless people. There are so many. I pretend I don't see them.

Loud noises still frighten me because of you.

I have stage fright but it always feels like a cop out when I admit to it.

I hate being categorized but I put everyone else into boxes, sometimes with fancy sparkly bows.

I try not to truly hate certain people but sometimes it's hard. I am glad I get along with most people.

I try to do good deeds and make an effort not to tell people about doing the good deed.

When I use paper towels I sometimes feel guilty and think about the beauty of fall.

I want to believe that idiots just have talents that lie elsewhere.

I imagine I will be the old neighbor that children flock to learn more about life outside their surrounding adults.

I want to buy everything I think my nieces would like in its adult size but then realize that it would be mean to buy everything they like for myself.

I secretly wish this will replace resume writing, so I no longer need to do job interviews.

Considerations for My Poetry

Check	Reference to high art forms
Check	Reference to famous artists
Check	Overanalysis
Check	At least one literary reference
Check	Puns and irony
Check	Room for discussion
Check	Empathetic
Questionable	Sense (Of the mind or the big five? Still questionable)
Questionable	Direction (More of a meandering stream)
Questionable	Audience appeal

Decidedly 70% Poetry. Math doesn't lie.

Imposter Syndrome

I am an artist
I enjoy creating
Sound, ideas, pictures.

Self rated C-listed poet
But nevertheless
I am what I choose to be.

They say there is truth in self affirmations.

We are each shouldering a boulder towards the top
It's hard to appreciate the journey when tired
But we still climb, crawl, grasp, hang
Falling is harder
But do you start over with the same boulder?
Do you ever think of the irony when running up a steep hill?
We eventually try to recover or actually recover
Slightly damaged but smarter with the ascent
Armed with new tools to compensate for weakness
Still hiding under a bright yellow hat.

Quarantine

My newest hobby while drinking
Is to love everyone and everything on twitter and instagram
Instead of at a bar with friends and strangers.

I've learned my weakness for art
I visit museums alone
Art is best in person
Creating or appreciating others' work
The perfection of imperfection
Or the perfection of attempted perfection
Such a beauty captured by each and every artist.

My closest friend at the moment is my room
I create, work, eat, drink, and live here
Surrounded by my Hawaiian art prints
A picture of Frida and a Basquiat quote
Lots of photos of my adorable nieces
The only lei I brought back to the mainland
Things that inspire me and things I love.

This is Me on TV

Catch me from my good side
Edit out what appears bad
Make myself more beautiful
Or hold a funhouse mirror
Delete that take.

I will say that for shock value
I want to see your reaction
The audience reaction
Experimentation to figure you out
While investigating your human values.

I will charm you and be pleasant
Speak of interesting facts and topics
As a Jill-of-many-trades
I hope you will give me attention in return
You know, people make money off of that
At least I try to entertain you
Engage you in discourse.

Self indulgent for curious ends.

We are not our thoughts
So are we our art,
Our behavior,
What we write,
Or what we say we are?

In front of [fill-in-the-blank]
Are you truly the same?
A filtered spectrum

Based on core values and beliefs.
Do you play life like chess
Or Whack-a-mole
Timing makes a difference
Making life brilliant
Of the infinite possibilities and outcomes.

Test all the parameters in your model
You will still get a statistic
For a web of series or events
You can and cannot control
Separate the logic from the emotion
And you may be successful
But failed as a value.

It is not black and white
Life is complex
We are complex
Call me Chartreuse.

Repetitive Machinery

<pre>
            This is Art
  This is Art   This is Art
   This is Art   This is Art   Is this hard
This is Art   This is Art   Is this hard
This is Art   This is Art   Is this Art   Is this hard
This is Art   Is this Art ... Is this Art Is this Art Is this hard
This is Art   This is Art   Is this Art Is this Art ... Is this hard   Is this hard
This is Art   This is Art   Is this Art Is this Art   Is this hard
This is Art   This is Art   Is this Art   Is this hard
  This is Art   This is Art   Is this Art   Is this hard
   This is Art   This is Art   Is this Art   Is this hard
     This is Art   This is Art   Is this Art   Is this hard
           This is Art This is Art   Is this Art   Is this hard
</pre>

Altered

What is math?
Math is all around us.

Who are you?
A good place to start is classic rock.

What makes you human?
We can make choices and think about alternative futures.

The above was co-authored by my phone.
Classic rock is okay.

Zombie Apocalypse

I've been told by multiple people that I would not survive a
    Zombie Apocalypse
In an attempt to prove wrong those who disbelieve in my
    survival, this is written proof of my survival …

The Basics:
1. I've taken boxing classes
2. I was born and raised in Atlanta, Georgia
3. Both give me more street cred than my small stature assumes
4. I have already started my endurance training

The Plan:
1. Steal a car on my block (so sorry to the person whom I'll have
    to knock out with one of my pans)
2. Drive to the coast, get on a boat, sail away to an isolated
    island. I would gain all knowledge on how to get to the coast
    and sailing from the internet - because everything is on the
    internet these days, and I'm good at learning
3: Prepped supplies: fire starter, machete, something warm, fresh
    water, food, tent

The Life:
1. Books to identify useful plants and to be my friends
2. I'd spend my days catching fish and scavenging for food,
    avoiding wild beasts, and becoming one with nature
3. At night, I'd try to create new creatures with star patterns.

Then after some time:
I would probably be killed by a cute poisonous frog living on the
    isolated island. Death by cuteness.
Technically I did survive the Zombie Apocalypse.

A Day of Abstract Art Inspiring More Abstract Art

Staring in Confoundment
Looking for something
To make sense
Or let it wash over you
Until it doesn't need to make sense
And let it be
This is the brain child of someone with purpose.

Of one particular piece
Taking a closer look
Noticing that the artist
A pioneer of using technology
For his time
Mixed copies into artwork from the 80's
A past time for us
While gone his legacy survives
And possibly will beyond
Past our own selves.

Sometimes the writing beside
The work conveys new meaning
Artist quotes are my favorite
Even when quoted
Is there even deeper meaning?
One artist said
No one will understand
In an infinite sense, he is ultimately correct
And that is a very lonely idea
However he fails to mention all those
Who see and will see his work
And tries.

Twirling in a tulle skirt
The clicking of white heels
Posing
For her boyfriend
With the long lens camera
To capture the best shot
From different angles
In front of Majerus's artwork
"What may look good today
May not look good tomorrow"
I do not miss the irony
In so many ways
New art with art
Like this as well.

The sounds
Like a siren
Mesmerized
Drawing me to skip rooms and rooms
Of masterpieces
To uncover the source
While intriguing
Ignorance was more blissful
Having been told the mystery
I imagined a greater story
To unfold before my eyes and ears
It came from a small television
In the corner
Like baby
With a plaque explanation
As a logically-minded individual
I was expecting mermaids.

John Cage

As we step onto the train
The percussion solo begins
With occasional piccolo improvisations
The person next to you turns and
Crinkles their newspaper
The teenager's headphones
Leak instrumental guitar sounds
Sporadic vocal lines appear
Another person across taps their foot
To their own beat with wooden soles
The intercom comes on
'The next stop is …'
The major third indicating
A stop
Doors open
More people scuffle inside
A singer-songwriter's voice
Wafts into the train
Boots against the floor
Bags against bags
Clothes against the seats
'Doors closing. Please step away from the doors.'
Descending major third
Doors try to close
Doors open
Descending major third
Doors close
A murmur of conversations
As the train begins again
Coins jingle from a beggar
'Can anyone spare some change?'

Coming closer
A kid trying to climb up the seat
To tap erratically on the windows
Peering outside into darkness
A dog whining softly
On its owner's lap
Descending major third
Doors open
We step off the train.

Spring

Whomever started
'everything in moderation'
Must have known about
Vivaldi's Spring.

Every time
I hear the first measure
I cringe in pain
Too much
I can't listen anymore
Internally
I duck in terror
Torture
Like
Nails on a chalkboard.
(Sorry if this is your favorite)

Spring is not 4/4
It does not walk
With both right arm and foot
Swinging simultaneously forward
…
Left arm and foot
Forward
Clunk
Like clogs awkwardly
Stomping across wooden floors.

It also does not
Repeat
Like a broken record

Each blade of grass
Is the same but different
Some variation
Fluid in length
Flies through the sky
With grace.

He illustrates
Literally
Birds, streams, storms
Sure,
the storm part
Is impressive
When done well
But this is still not spring
Or my type of spring.

Idée fixe

I was struck straight into the heart
By Amor's arrow
When I heard the
Smooth baritone's song
Floating through the air
To find my heart.

The mesmerizing voice
Took over my thoughts
Blindingly searching
For the person
With the voice.

I languished as
Days became nights
Nights became years
No memory of time
With my obsession
Of his voice.

When I finally awoke
I was at death's open door
Ready to rest
And give up my dream
And then I heard.

The Joy of Crunch

There is something special
About walking through a pile
Of freshly raked leaves
Your entire foot goes through
As if there was nothing there
Inconsequential
Except the beautiful sounds
Of crunching.

It is not unlike
Finding and eating
Small sweet potato fries pieces
At the bottom of the box
Or the sounds of granola clusters
Disintegrated by your teeth
These are still fulfilling in a sense.

Outside of autumn
Gravel could be
A potential replacement
But not as satisfying
Pebbles can get stuck
On the bottom of your shoe
And falling would not
Be a nice sensation.

SAD

Autumn teases us - With ravishing beauty - Fresh breezes -
Gentle sunlight.

Only to
Fall
Into winter.

Clouds gather - Bringing darkness - All around
Days shorter - Than eyes open - Stuck in black
Trees naked - Freezing outside
The ground - Stripped
Of life.

In the Corner

There's a dark figure
Lurking
Waiting
For the opportune moment
To seize me by the throat
Squeeze all essence out.

I must keep one eye
Watching
The forever game
Green light Red light
Except there is no winner
Only darkness.

I sense the tricks
Played on my mind
Doubts and hesitation
Playing on sensitivity
Reminding of what was
Or could be.

Even in blinding light
The corner is still dark
Smaller
But I can feel the frigid flares
An eternal flame
A harbinger of danger.

I remember the cold claws
Violently slashing my heart
The biting frost searing

Through my skin
While darkness
Cracks into my skull.

I fight, kick, push
And lose control
Only when I stop
I have strength
And
Push back
In the corner.

Struggle

Flowers dull
With a daily stale taste
Surrounded by white noise
And stillness
Robotic wake up
Work, go home,
Sleep.

When you close your eyes
Nothing
No dreams
Dragging yourself
Inside an endless cave
You open your eyes
Nothing
No direction
No answer
Heaving your weight
In some nameless direction
While bleeding blisters
Swell at your feet
No pain.

Your heart ticks
But no longer works
No recollection of a life
Outside the tunnel
Alive yet dead
An unsettling balance
Easier to end
Harder to escape.

In the blankness
Something catches
Your attention
A seed you swallow
That takes root in your heart
It starts to hurt
You slowly awaken
You notice food left out
For You
To nourish your soul
It's painful
You begin to feel burden
Deep within your bones
But you smell
The crispness of a new day
Sense nameless hues that
Glow around you
Sparkling laughter
Settling in your heart.

Everyday you wander
Search for water
To grow
Survive
Even a handful of mud
Can be what
Makes life worthy
Smoothes your feet
Your pain
Nurturing takes effort
But over time
You learn

What is best
For yourself in order
To blossom
In your
Own uniqueness.

Always a light

She stands alone
With a torch
Throughout the night
In the fiercest of weathers
For us to look towards
Her light.

The flash of
Lightning bugs
At dusk
To find each other
But for you
To find a way.

The glow inside
The ocean
By the smallest
Of creatures
Our hands
Cannot hold.

Even in the darkest of forests
You can climb
To see the endless
Sky of stars
Infinite glowing galaxies.

Lighted
Empty city streets
Without a soul nearby
Providing direction

You even see
Your neighbor left
Their porch light
To light
Your way home.

Wind chimes

Like
tinkling laughter
Of a child

Ephemeral and
Evanescent
To my senses.

Wishing
For constant
Breeze.

Hands

It's sad
To think
That T-rexes
Could not
Hold hands.

No way to
Reach another
Without
Violent slashing.

Instead
I like
To draw dinosaurs
Giving each other
Hearts
For a happier life.

Euphoria

I step outside into the quiet city
A bright and new morning
Sunshine everywhere
Across the open fields in the park
My heart is warmed and free
It skips across the green grass
Laughs, surprised, at the ducks quacking
And the other strange noises near the water.

I wake up to see you
A gentle smile, happy with beautiful dreams
You pull me closer in your warm arms
Hearing both our heartbeats at once
Different beats but working as one
It is just the two of us
On this island
As the outside world melts away.

I hear the introduction and three notes
I inhale a calm deep breath
And begin '*Quando m'en 'vo ...*'
Notes float radiantly out
As I see the sound dance
Surround me in open space
I feel
Beauty from my head down to my toes.

Colorfully

If I could blow my good thoughts
Like dandelion seeds
Would the joy be contagious?

I could infiltrate all the pristine lawns
Create some chaotic happiness
Yellow flowers in a sea of serious green.

Jagged against curved anonymity
Bold while gently growing
Living life colorfully.

The Perfect Lawn

The grass is always greener
But once we dig deeper
The green could be a bit more yellow
The yellow a bit more brown
With some new regrowth.

Would it be worthwhile
If it were a walk in the park?
They say plants grow better with cow shit
I guess you'd get some nice green grass
With a large pile of shit then.

Ocean

I had a conversation
With a professor once
About the duality
Of the ocean
That made it
Extra special.

While beautiful
And vast
Its power can be
Terrifying.

I was pulled inside a wave once
So easily
Dragged under water and flipped
I emerged shaken and choking
Salt water and sand
Everywhere
I remember this like yesterday
I still go into the ocean
As it calls to me.

I used to go to the beach
Alone at dusk
The changes in scenery
And sounds created
Captivating serenity
The last rays of sun
Reflected across the ocean
Curious popping noises
Coming from the water's edge

Sharing secrets of the night
Each evening
The same place but
Different story.

Rain

So cliche
And dramatic
Personified
As heavenly tears
From dark skies
I am also a victim of this image.

The antagonist of the story
Creating obstacles
Increasing the baggage
From every direction.

Of intense joy
Singing, and Dancing,
Igniting mischief
For those passing by.

Overcast in large shadows
Drops sounding against pavement
A friend who empathizes
Understands without words.

Nature's worth

While shopping online for dresses, I found
A small bundle of twigs
Discounted from $50 to $30
There was no indication as to the type of tree
Or any special qualities of the branches
Just that they were white and on sale
And appeared in the middle of a page of clothes.

In second grade, I brought my teacher
A bundle of azaleas from my front yard
A few weeks later, I found a beautiful plant
I plucked it from my lawn to give to her as well
But the kids on the bus made fun of me
For carrying around a weed
(I believe it was a nut grass to be exact)
So I tossed the grass out in disappointment.

Value

Sometimes
It's much easier to see
The worth of others
Than to see yourself

We are all human
But
We are also all different

We have shared experiences
But
We have unique perspectives

We set our own standards
To measure our own worth.

Would we set those
Same standards
For a loved one?

Independent Women Pt. 808

Tell me I'm beautiful
I already am.

Change my car's flat tire
I can change it myself.

Laugh at my jokes
I'm fucking funny.

Buy me diamonds and flowers
I can buy them myself.

Luxuriously wine and dine me
I eat and drink anything really.

I don't need you to complete me
I'm already very whole
I guess the others
Could be a nice gesture.

Bad Subway Story

Dearest Subway,

You open doors to amazing and new places
Yet you close doors in my face while looking straight into my
    eyes
Even when I've run as fast as I can after you.

You take me to places farther than my feet can carry me
Yet make me walk even farther when I get there
Why do you tease me so?

Why are you never on time?
Is it me or is it you?

I hate to admit
I do need you more than you need me.

I can only stay away from you for up to a day
But I still come straight back.

This sounds like an abusive relationship.
Let's break up.

Fight

Do not
Undermine my abilities
Speak condescendingly
Laugh at this type of behavior

As one
That can
Carry and create life
How does that make
Us
Physically and Mentally
Weaker?

Are you so intimidated
That I speak my mind
I own up to my emotions
As a human being
Or that I can comprehend
Much more than you wanted?

It only became an issue
When you belittled me
And tried to box me
Into an ignorant trope

I am
Enraged
By your Sexism.

Cathartic Times

I yell and scream
On top of this building
Obscenities
Fiery words
Smashing mirrors
Plates, bowls
Glasses, vases
Against
The cement walls
Then leap off
The building
Into the air
To release
This energy …

To land
Cat-like and
Walk off
As if this
All never happened.

Lines

Waiting in line
Is a funny idea
A cafe named Winner
Down the street from me
Is winning
People will wait
Extremely long hours for
Food like ramen burgers
Entertainment like roller coasters
Museums like the Louvre
Retail like sample sales
Once in a lifetime experiences
But the wait is
Time exchanged
Sometimes including money.

Each person has a
Different waiting threshold
I didn't wait for ramen burgers
But I did wait for a shrimp truck
My maximum threshold
Usually 30 minutes
Unless its art museums
Or voting
I spent over 3 hours
That is equivalent to 1.5 movies
Waiting with a friend is better
Anticipation loves company.

Cause for Confusion

The word
Fuck
Has many meanings.

My roommate yells
'I want to fuck her'
I get so confused
And shocked
By hearing
My definition.

But she continues to complain
And is very angry
And so then I realize
The usage of the word.

Where is everyone?

I could be speaking to you
Looking at those small brown specks
Inside your irises
I see you, you see me
Clearly
We are both somewhere else.

Beautiful plates of food
Greens, yellows, browns, reds,
Flawlessly plated
Colorful drinks with orchids
Moonlight reflecting off the glass
I look at their dinner table
They look at their screens.

We are closer
Than we have ever been in life
A video away
A message
Yet even more isolated
Everything is fighting for you
Pay attention to me
We never talk on the phone anymore
When you say words have weight.

In the city of New York
Full of strangers
We are inside little cubby holes
I sing inside my nest
Loving the anonymity
But at the same time

Miss that I am sharing you
My soul
Are you listening?

Little Lending Library

Down my street
You sit perched
On the ledge
Strong, wooden
With glass doors.

You open
To a new world
Which are you?
Loved, hated
Used, abused
Outdated, forgotten
Bestseller, obscure
Classic, memoir
Foreign, educational
How long will you stay?
And will you ever return?

As a travel guide
Have you been
To those places
Your words explore?
Or are you a guide
Of unmet dreams
And hopes?
Were you owned
By someone
Who wants to share
Your wealth of knowledge?

Your doors
Open and close
So frequently
Your own story
Unwritten
But through others.

Chasing Happiness

Blinded by the rush
The extra high
We run towards
A false ambition.

We tire
And then realize
In retrospect
That running
Was the thing
We were
Searching.

We are driven by
Tangible
Results
When we finally
Rest
The meaning
Becomes apparent.

Lost and Found

I found you
Covered in dirt
On the side of the road
Abandoned
Once loved and cherished
Forgotten and abused
What happened to you?

I will love you
Shelter you from harm
As you are important
Show you kindness
That you have craved
From others
I will nurture you
Watch you grow
Into a beautiful orchid.

Weakness

Under a tall shadow
Always chasing
A standard drifting off
When guaranteed a spot
On the last boat off the island

Isolated, useless, abandoned
Blindly clawing at invisible enemies
Closing the door from the world
Alone
Swallowed whole inside a hurricane
Directionless in circles
Turning to a knife
To take care of the mess
To prevent more of a mess
Lost in mindless reason.

Too soft to continue
Too weak to stay
A constant indecision
Unable to to live fully
A waking nightmare
Somehow knowing
These same qualities
Prevailed.

Unlucky

I saw a black cat
As I walked under a ladder
The same night
The grim reaper
Appeared sitting next
To me at dinner.

I should have known
the next morning
I woke up to the
Pounding sound
Of my window blinds
Banging the walls
From the howling wind
I push to get up
Fighting against
The wall of air
To close the windows.

A moment of silence
Once shut out
Then glass shatters
And the Storm
Arrives inside.

My eyes reopen to
Whiteness
I hear the storm
from a distance
I sense the cutting winds
But I am surrounded

In blankness
How do I get out?
Trapped within
A storm
But inside white space.

I run in circles
To find an exit
Scream my lungs raw
Slap my arms red
To return.

Once I tire
I fall asleep
To open my eyes
Again.

Addict

Measures to cope
To ease the burden
The weight of living
Of slipping control
A jaded blur
With no worry
A pill of forgetfulness
A shot of relief
To inject the black hole
With something that fills
A satisfied fullness
Apart from outside
Sparking
An explosion of
Glorious adventures
Fresh dreams
New life
Into one that is
Already living
Once awake
The fantasy forgotten
Wax ripped off
The burn is fresh
Upon red flesh
Blistering with pus
The ditch deepens
In search of
New bandage
To hold together
The tiny seeds poured
Into a steel colander.

Death

A world of infinite

Silence

Empty

Nothingness.

So many
Moving photographs
Fading with time
Fading with you.

Trains keep running
Time has stopped
While reassessing
The worth of
Fleeting pricelessness.

The sun lessens
A darkness settles
The wound
Slowly
Feasters and heals
Until the pain
With seasons
Becomes normal.

A scar that
Affects you
Forever.

Just Breathe

Breathing inspires
It's not a coincidence
It is what keeps us alive
That makes it so
Dramatic and Enchanting
At the same time.

The simpleness of breathing
With extreme consequences
We have experienced

The urgency of no air.

The intimacy of shared air.

The calmness of a deep breath.

The ease of released breath.

The beauty that could change breath.

The discomfort of blocked air.

The shared experience
Makes for even a greater connection
An instinctual understanding
Between us all
And
Enriches the experience of a breath.

Time

Laughter is retrospective
As time is present
So if you think about
Living in the moment
You are actually
Thinking of the past.
If you are pondering
The previous words
You are also
Thinking of the past.
What is is was.

Is it circular?

I just want warm hugs
Not ones where you greet someone
Like being in polite society
Ones where you and the other person feel
This is a hug
I'm giving you my warm feelings
I appreciate you as a person.
Apparently it's an American thing
To greet people with 'how are you?'
Because it is considered polite
But are you actually asking
Or being polite?
I am guilty of this as well.
If I am not having a good day
I still smile and be cheery
I lie, 'I'm doing fine'
I laugh at everything
I am a ball of pleasantry
It is so so so much effort
I get so tired
The entire time, I think about
Snuggling under my blankets
The softness of my sheets
The warmness of my pillows
But sometimes you
Will be contagious
And make my day better.
Then I think about my efforts
To be cheery, ask, hug
Hopefully it's paid forward.

Writing Dreams

Sapping through my fingertips
I am afraid this is my Frühe Jahr
My nutrients
Vitamin C for you, And for you,
Maintain that brightness.

Potassium so this remains strong
E so this skin is so clear, it's transparent
B so two eyes open to three
Protein to stay grounded
These fingerprints blossom like the Deer God's footprints
Eventually dying away to new saplings.

Message in a Bottle

I cannot wait to imagine
This life beyond my hands.

It will sit next to bestsellers
Inside of a lending library
To be flipped through
Occasionally by a passerby
Then shredded for fire
To keep people warm for the winter
Snuggling in front of their fireplace.

It will sit on a shelf for years to come
Covered in coughing induced dust
Only to be discovered by a youngster
Who will be inspired to create
Art from its pages.

It will be read on repeat
Dog-eared pages
Light pencil markings
Wrinkled pages
From excess use
Specific pages torn out
Loved in its form.

It will be donated
To a used bookstore
Where it will stay hidden
Among treasures of books
Finally finding a permanent home
To settle. *So much potential in a life.*

Reasonable

So many paths to choose
Which one is right
Follow your gut
Or follow your brain.

I don't make decisions
I know I will regret
But is that
The Right Choice?

In retrospect
I see where I've been
To step forward
Is still a shot in the dark.

Not moving is
A big waste of time
Where should I go?
What should I do?

I typically
Have my choices
Stolen from me
If I wait too long.

I cannot settle for less
But what will I lose
In an effort
To try for more?

What will I gain
Carving a new path?
Will I be blinded
By the million possibilities
That I don't see
What is best
What is worth the risk
For my choices?

Is this regret?

If I mailed you a letter
With all my complicated feelings
Would our relationship change
For the better?
I'm not a great writer
I'm just honest
Maybe too honest
But I can never have
Those important conversations
Because those memories
Have burnt into ashes
But scarred onto my soul
I have forgiven but can't forget
Does that make a difference
In the long run?
Is this the end
I have to accept?

Conundrum

Aware of existence
Trying to live life lightly
With all its ironies
To a larger extent
Life's purpose
Dependent on beliefs
Based on ideas
Can we knock everything
Off of the table
And just be?

Black, White, Grey

My heart becomes overstuffed

With the cruelty of the world
That it bursts into a stagnant state
I can see dust particles passing my eyes
My entire body pulls towards the ground
And I lay in a petrified state
Unable to think and feel
A viscous mantra that keeps me going
Until the pain becomes normalized.

With the glorious beauty of human nature
The joy one brings to another
Boundaries pushed and successes in the world
My love then given and taken freely
Good thoughts and intentions passed on
My eyes squint from the brightness
The warmth given to my core
Feeling grounded yet flying at once.

Dubious nature of ideas which root
From tradition, consequence
The confusion of what to accept
Or not to accept at all
Uncomfortable standing in a room full of chairs
Unable to take sides when complexities overload
Hesitant while pulled in different directions
Attempting to sit at the center of balance.

MD

It crushes me to see your lack of hope
Hard eyes from witnessing too much
A dark cynical outlook on life
The end decided with no control
A dullness unable to be shined
Even if you are making a difference
Small now but grows only slowly with time
The daily damage takes a larger toll
Blinding you from the small joys.

I wish I could do something to fix everything
Or at least fix something
But it's not so simple
I cannot help you in this new normal
If only I could give you a piece of my hope
For a better future, would your eyes change?
I appreciate you
Your efforts and determination
But what can I do for you?
I feel just as helpless as those haunting eyes.

Conqueror

Oppressing humidity
Onslaught of dark clouds
Wind whipping across the field
The intensity as a preview
Anticipation creating anxiety
Of oncoming annihilation
A waste of reinforcements
Developed on limited time
Resorting to prayer
Hiding within shells
As all else will be lost
Mindless repetition
Free will transforms into art
Disappearing into mind.

Trap

A vicious cycle
Innocuous seeds
Grow into hand grenades
Perpetuating stereotypes
Forced into those truths
Empty-handedly
Trying to go against the grain
Assaulted on all paths
Except for no choice.
Hands, so many hands
From a sinking island
Bound for the worst
Hands given to hold
In death and in pain
The masses have spoken
Repeatedly
When will it be enough?

Why can't we just get along?

By fault, I am a romantic
I have these ideas
We can all just get along
By agreeing to disagree.

One bad apple in a basket
Doesn't mean you should throw it all out
Cut away the bad parts
And you see still an apple
It's still edible
Also,
why would you put a fully rotten apple
In the basket in the first place?
I did double check,
Eating a particularly bad apple could poison you.

I guess that didn't work too well
With my main point
Because the rotten apples are still apples
You would leave them on the ground.

But if we were to be in my world
We would leave the rotten apples
Add nutrients and care
To create new apples to pick
Next season.

Yes, a romantic indeed.

What kind of person am I?

I admire heroes. These people have a fast, natural reaction when others are put in danger. A child, no less than 8 years old, has the ability to try to save his classmates during a violent school shooting. What was going through that child's mind at the moment? Did they even know exactly what they were doing? Was it their innate goodness that reacted that way?

Then I think about my own reaction in these types of situations. How would I react? What about those who are frozen in fear or escape? We know that this is not wrong in terms of reaction, but I fear that I may be one of them. I have a want to be that good person; it doesn't need to be a hero situation.

Moral of the story: We can all try to be better people but still be kind to those who fail daily.

Body Parts

My brain is disconnected from my body
I regularly bump into things
My head is full of these thoughts
And I run into everything
I'm not in the moment
Always forward or backwards.

Good to overanalyze both directions
Bad to live that way
We get so caught up in our thoughts
Thoughts of work, people, …things
Thoughts of thoughts, like me right now.

I like when I run and I hit a point where I cannot think
I hear birds, the trees, my body
Instinctively, I keep going
Is this living in the moment?
But the quietness is comforting.

We apparently obtain 60% of information visually
My body parts are apparently not part of the 60%
It takes extra effort to try to even out the percentage
Shouldn't it be 20%?
And even so, not everyone has the option for an even 20%
It would be interesting to try
Let's say we sleep for 6 hours, that is one fourth of the day
Then closing our eyes for 12 hours while awake
Would that be like 25% visual information gathering?
I guess then
I would be able to sense those chairs and walls coming.

New Normal

Draw a triangle entitled a Square
When did we become so serious?
White fences lined neatly
Instead of canvasing open fields
Hard times call for hardness
Seep some sparkling water
To hydrate and awaken life
From its cold and frigid form.

Slowly rotting from outside tragedy
Is unnatural
It cannot go unnoticed yet
Cannot be fully consumed
A delicate responsibility ensues
Per person
Between practicality and curiosity
A confinement limited by the mind.

My friends have become 0s and 1s
Disconnected from my present time
Yet the only latch onto this existence
The intangible
A retroactive living of one's life
To present more clarity on living.

Backscatter

A genial Picasso peers out
An attempt to do good
But without proper reception
Misconnects, misunderstood
A facade juxtaposed with its interior.

Worst thoughts based on appearance
Accepting assumptions
From an ugly scarred past
The awkward pieces of this puzzle are all present
Can you please accept all the parts?

A daily struggle for Aphrodite's perfection
Out and inside
This impression offends unintentionally
Could you please
Try to look beyond preconceptions?

To Dickinson

I'm nobody
Who are you
Why cannot I be me
When I have a mind of my own
Why can't we just be nobodies
Who can choose ourselves
When we are ready to face the crowd?

Last Judgement

Scoop out my heart
Let it splatter
Into a Rorschach Test
What do you see?

Complexities
Lots of dry humor
Lots of trying
Lots of failing
Melancholy
Love
Kindness
Hope
No Regrets

What's next?